Times Getting Hard: Scriptures Of Comfort For Hard Days

Johannes Tefo

Published by Johannes Tefo, 2024.

Also by Johannes Tefo

Family spiritual Warfare Books
Youth's Guide To Spiritual Warfare
A Women's Guide To Spiritual Warfare

Standalone
Deliver Your Soul From Evil
Overcoming Spirit Of Stagnation
The 24: Prophetic Word For This Season 2024 And Beyond
Michael For Warfare
Territorial Spirits: Overcome Evil Strongholds in Your Life And
Take Over Your Community With Strategic Warfare And
Winning Prayers
Prayers Against Suicide Spirit
Spiritual Warfare When Enough is Enough
Identity In Christ
Prayers Against Satanic Networks
The Workplace You Need: Spiritual Warfare Prayers That
Silence Evil Powers At Your Workplace.

Deliverance From Mind Control: Be Free And Delivered From Every Marine Demons Of Mind Control
Times Getting Hard: Scriptures Of Comfort For Hard Days

Table of Contents

I dedicate this book to friends and family. God is bigger than our problems. Take heart. Be courageous in the name of the Lord!

Times getting Hard.

These days you will hear this term often "We are living in the end times". Even non-believers and those who are called atheists attest that our generation is different from generations before. And it is the real truth, times are getting harder and harder. That we have to develop a thick skin. With so much at our disposal, there is so much that can bring us down. New technology is emerging. The world is turning into robotic. While it is a good thing, it also comes with shortfalls. In the days of Noah, there were giants at that time—the hybrid of Angels and humans, called Nephilim.

Even in our day, we are not alone. People in other parts of the world have started mingling with robots. Besides that, the gods of old have returned. We can see through the pattern in culture, tradition, and religious worship. This is the day of all-time high deception. People a deceived. People are going to be deceived. Even the elect of God. Deception is a serious deadly weapon of the end times stemming from the kingdom of darkness. There has always been a conflict between the children of light and the children of the darkness.

But we all know that in the end, light shall prevail. As the Almighty God rose up in the times of Moses, so shall He arise in our time. When God arises, His enemies fall. When God arises, it is a sign of victory. When you read Mathews 24, you can see with your own eyes the prophecies of Jesus Christ unfolding. Rumors of wars are everywhere. Famine has hit the land. Many have received the word from the Lord about global famine, and so am I. It is part and parcel of Mathews 24 prophecies. I will urge you to study this scripture with diligence—allowing the Holy Spirit to unveil the mystery of these prophecies.

The first thing Christ said "*Take heed that no man deceives you*". This statement is bigger than the famine, wars, pestilence etc. when you are deceived, it can only take God to take the evil blinders out of your mind and eyes. It pains even the most because deception is already in the body of Christ. Deception it's a spiritual evil roots that has to be uprooted. The truth of the Word of Christ is that which set the captives free.

If you attend many of Charismatic prophetic churches, you will know what deception looks like. But again, not all of them. In the body of Christ, it is the doctrine issue. It is more like a man straying away from the teaching of Christ and Apostles, incorporating other religious dogma of healing and teaching. We see this from African brothers and sisters who are leading masses into doctrines of the devils.

there shall be famines, and pestilences, and earthquakes, in divers places.
8 All these are the beginning of sorrows.

If you feel like what has happened and what is happening is enough, it is just the beginning. The first weapon of the devil is mass deception to stray many away from the godly path of righteousness. He is fighting to capture many souls from going to the Father at the end of the age. In the realm of the spirit, it is the fight of the gods and goddess. Princes has rose up fighting the anointed and mocking God himself. Cheer up, the Lord God has chosen Zion! We are the Sons and daughters of Mount Zion, built not by men but by the mighty spirit of God. The Lion from the tribe of Judah has triumph.

This roaring lion that is devouring, shall be defeated and overcome by the blood of the lamb. Trust the Lord God till the end of the race, you shall not be ashamed. Ours it is He that created the heavens and the earth. The famine, the pestilences, all kinds of diseases, floods, and earthquakes shall be in diver places, as the Lord God delivered Noah, so shall He deliver His own who has covered themselves by the mighty blood of Christ.

Even Enoch, prophesized of the days like these. He is the man who saw Christ before he was known. The life of Enoch is an epitome of faith that never dry out—faith strengthened by the mighty spirit of God. Again, it is to show us that God is the refuge of those who believe in Him. As it is written in the scriptures that Enoch was not because God took Him.

Psalm 9:9 The LORD also will be a refuge for the oppressed, a refuge in times of trouble.

A life of faith is a different path. A lonely one, a stranger, a sojourner in the land like the prophets and saints of old. History repeats itself, if they persecuted Elijah, they are going to persecute you for bearing the name of the Lord. Usually troubles mount up when you are all about God's business, but the Lord shall deliver you out of all the trouble.

Psalm 34:19 Many are the afflictions of the righteous: but the LORD delivereth him
out of them all.
20 He keepeth all his bones: not one of them is broken.

The righteous are bound to go through the storms but they will come out the other side in the name of Jesus. We grow in spiritual wisdom when challenges multiples, God drops light in our mind to come up with solutions that will benefit us for the rest of our lives.

In this book, I have included the scriptures of comfort and hope for you when times get hard. We go through the storms in our families, marriages, at workplace, at church etc. The Word of God is the sword of the spirit at the heart of evil kings. We wrestle with principalities and powers of darkness that will try to keep us in bondage. Some of the things we go through stem from spirit world. As matured faith people, we should already know that spiritual warfare is real. We are contending with the prince of this world who will do anything to deceive us.

We should never lose hope in the Lord. Keep the faith in the name of Jesus Christ. In your homes, let the high praises of God be in your mouth. You were created to worship the God Most High. Already we breath the name of the DNA of God.

Jesus Christ is our perfect example. As He fought Satan through the Word of God. Likewise, the same principles still apply—it is written! If you do not know the Word of God, you cannot argue your case with the enemy, he will defeat you. The Devil knows the Word from genesis to revelation. We are no match to the angels, even to the fallen angels. But through the holy spirit of God, we shall always mount up with wings like eagle's and fly.

Isaiah 40:31 But they that wait upon the LORD shall renew their strength; they shall
mount up with wings as eagles; they shall run, and not be weary; and they shall
walk, and not faint.

You need the spirit of patience to wait upon the Lord. The spirit of patience is one of the fruits of the spirits. Abraham rested on the promises of God, acted on them, and believed them. Hold on unto what God has promised you. Faith is believing the promises of God laid out in the bible. God sees it as an act of righteousness when you believe. Believe, you shall receive.

The scripture says that *"But they that Wait upon the Lord shall renew their strength"*. To renew is to repeat what was already there. It means new strength, new visions, new dream, and new perspective of looking at things. You will start seeing things from God's point of view. Mountains will become small boys to you. You shall rise above challenges. Most of all, you shall be above darkness, which is the kingdom of Satan in this case.

Eagles fly high above the clouds. And they have sharp eyes that sees miles away. In the bible it is associated with the prophetic nature or office of the prophet. Wait upon the Lord, you shall be filled with spiritual knowledge, wisdom, and understanding of God. This goes beyond the ministry, in all aspect of your endeavor you shall prosper. Prosperity is the name of the game for the righteous in the Lord.

Words of Encouragement.

When you are in dry season in your life, the must drink water must be the Word of God for that season. Words are spirit and life. Thet give life to your weakening soul. The most important person in this world is your inner man. You spirit man need the covering of the light of God.

God is your source of strength. God is the Father of all souls. All humans are bound to fall at some point, however, through the excellency of the name of the Lord we shall arise. When men arise, it is because the light has come. The light of God is power, strength, and wisdom. Spiritual understanding of things comes from the Lord.

Daniel and his friends survived through in Babylon because they sought the Lord with all their might, be it prayer, fasting, or humility. When God is number one in your life expect the world to be against you. Even your own family, at some point they are going to question your faith. Eventually, the chosen shall arise and shine. The chosen are the inheritor of the kingdom of God.

Daniel saw the increase in information in the last days when you read chapter 12. We are that generation that Daniel foresaw long ago. There is revolution in technology. The Word of God is everywhere. On social media, websites, television, and mass media overall.

We allow the Holy Spirit even in this day and age to lead. It also comes with a perfect opportunity to evangelize the gospel. Since it is written that this gospel must reach unto the end of the world before the end comes.

It is also through the grace of God that this book reaches you. I feel like when im inspired by the Word, my brethren, should also taste and see the goodness of the Lord. More than anything, we are called to be the witness. John was the first to witness the glory of God in Christ. We are like John, called to behold him.

The Psalmist says "They looked unto him, and were lightened: and their faces were not ashamed.Psalm:34:5".

Look unto Jesus Christ the hope of your glory. Look unto Jesus Christ, the perfect example of all the saints, living or dead. In Christ, we shall never be ashamed. Our names are written in the book of life. Our names are written in the book of destinies. Like Joshua was told "Be strong and of good courage". Be strong in the name of the Lord. Find strength and be comforted in the Lord.

1. *Psalm 23:1 - "The Lord is my shepherd; I shall not want."*

When times are getting hard, pockets are low, it's a life of living below minimum wage, pressure and depression cripple many, especially those who are not strong enough in their faith to handle the reality. This is the days where depression, suicide and death are taking the tall of all time high. The prophecies of old are unfolding, we are already hearing of the rumors of wars (Mathews 24). With all this, we have to be courageous like Joshua when stepping into the prophetic office of Moses.

The eyes of the Lord are upon the righteous, those who believe like Abraham did. As I always say, the spiritual deadly weapon of the end times is deception, hopelessness and depression. When the enemy can get you to see your God as small, he has won you. Never be shaken. The righteous are bold like lion. Like Judah, let the high praises of God be in your mouth even in difficult times. Praise is the weapon of warfare. If you want to bring own the ancient evil altars that are speak ill about you and your lineage, praise your way through, you shall see the light of the glory of God.

I have seen the hand of the Most High God moving in my life when I incorporate praise as the form of worship. He inhabits the praises of His people. He descends in a majestic way when the aura of worship ascends as sweet aroma unto His nostril. When the burned sacrifice of Noah went up, it felt good, then HE swore not to destroy humanity with floods again. When you see a rainbow, it is a symbol of the covenant of God and the righteous Noah that He will never again bring flood to end humanity.

Psalm 23 is the most famous scripture in the bible, yet powerful. It is a reminder to you that you are not alone. You have a mighty God who think good thoughts about you. Who think of you highly than any being on this planet. The shepherd leads the sheep. God is your FATHER, LEADER and your DELIVERER. King David boasted in the Lord 'My shepherd'. This is not a light statement, ancient people used to brag and boast about their God or gods especially when they are fighting. Any war that you a fighting in your life, brag about Christ to the devil. When the name of Christ is mentioned, all falls down. Kingdom comes tumbling down like tent hit by storms.

I will urge you to personalize this psalm and make it your own. Decree it when you are at home, meditate on it and pray it. It will strengthen your heart. All the issues of this life comes from your heart. If you hear is weak, you will fall. Let the mighty spirit of God strengthens you. If it be by your might, you are bound to be defeated. Trust in the Lord, it shall be well with your soul.

Your soul worth more than the currency of this world. Never sell your soul for temporary pleasures. Allow God in due time to make a way for you. The blessings of the Lord will make you rich, you and your children, even generation after you. And the blessings of the Lord add no sorrow. Everything that does not come with peace in your life doesn't not come from the Lord. Jesus Christ is not an author of confusion. He has left you with the mighty counselor—the Holy spirit to lead you and guide in all your ways. Stay blessed!

He binds the broken wounds!

1. *Psalm 34:18 - "The Lord is nigh unto them that are of a broken heart; and saveth such as be of a contrite spirit."*

We are bound to be broken while in this broken world. Many of us are from broken families. There are millions of thing that can bring your soul down. The road is not all glory and all blissful—the righteous shall encounter the same challenges Jesus encountered and the Apostles. The enemy is challenging the foundation, Christ, through us, by hurting us, dividing us, and manipulating us.

Marriage has collapsed. Families no longer in contact. There is so much that is going on but the Lord is still the king of this business. He is close to the cry of the righteous. In this case, the righteous are those who are counted by believing the gospel of Christ. Abraham believed, and it was counted to Him righteousness. Believe in the Lord you shall not be ashamed. And also, you shall not be moved. Storms, winds and floods shall come, but the Lord shall lift up the standard.

When the Lord God lift up the standard, you shall be above your enemies. You shall not drown in the deep sea of water but your head shall be above the water. He gives angels charge over you to walk with you, protect you and bless you. He also gives you light of understanding to be able to come up with divine solution to problems. Like Daniel the prophet, he walked in spirit of excellency that the whole kingdom of Babylon will wait for Daniel to lead them in spiritual matter. Daniel was above highly ranked witches and wizards of his time. Yet a humble soul that gives credit only the God of his salvation. Humility is a way to heart of God.

The right hand of my righteousness.

1. *Isaiah 41:10 - "Fear thou not; for I am with thee: be not dismayed; for I am thy God: I will strengthen thee; yea, I will help thee; yea, I will uphold thee with the right hand of my righteousness."*

From this scripture above, there a seven things that God promises you:

1. Fear not
2. I am with you.
3. Be not dismayed.
4. I am your God.
5. I will strengthen you.
6. I will help you.
7. I will uphold you with my right hand of my righteousness.

Fear keeps us from fully functioning in the office of faith. As faith pleases your God, this is what He has to say to you "Fear not". You cannot realize your full potential when fear is crippling you. By the way, fear is the opposite of faith. Substitute fear with faith. Now, how to walk in faith? Faith is the believe of the heart. You strengthen it by confession, proclamation and by declaration of scriptures. When you ingest and chew the Word of God, faith erupt like volcano.

The WORD is the sword of the spirit. Faith is a spiritual matter since it comes from your heart.

*Romans 10:9 That if thou shalt confess with thy mouth the Lord
Jesus, and shalt believe
in thine heart that God hath raised him from the dead, thou shalt
be saved.
10 For with the heart man believeth unto righteousness; and with
the mouth
confession is made unto salvation.
11 For the scripture saith, Whosoever believeth on him shall not be
ashamed.*

Believe in the name of Jesus Christ you shall not be ashamed. The excellency of the name of Christ has brought deliverance in my life, and in the life of my family. Joshua says to the children of Israel "choose from today whom you shall serve, as me and my family, we shall serve the Lord". People of God, worship only the Lord God Almighty through the mighty name of Christ, you shall be saved.

Along the journey, you can encounter gods and goddess that will promise you the world but at the end it leads to destruction and damnation. Allow the right victorious hand of the mighty God to deliver you from the power of evil. Allow the love of God to lead you and to walk in the humble spirit of meekness and repentance at all times. Allow correction and conviction from the Holy Spirit.

Whatsoever you need is in the hand of the Most High. Wealth, riches, honor, power, grace, happiness, and above all, abundancy of peace of mind—all these are in the court of the house of God. It is written that the righteous shall flourish in the court of the house of God.

When times gets hard, we should prayer hard. All the greatest men of God in the bible learned the art of prayer mastery through their spiritual journey. Prayer is a powerful tool. With all kinds of prayer, we should come before the Lord. While also not neglecting faith, faith moves mountain. You will have surprised that Jesus Christ emphasized faith more than anything in his ministry. As we have discussed, faith is an act of righteousness. Keep the faith, and keep moving forward!

1. *Matthew 11:28 - "Come unto me, all ye that labour and are heavy laden, and I will give you rest."*

The yoke of Jesus Christ is light unlike the yoke of men. Christ is the emblem of grace, love, mercy and faith. Incline your ear, and come unto Christ, your soul shall live. The teaching of Christ are anointed with power of God to breaks every yoke. It is the anointing that breaks yokes. The word Christ means "Anointed One".

Let the anointed one anoint you with fresh olive oil. Come unto the house of prayer, His house is called the house of prayer. He is the reviver of souls. The restorer of men. In life, there a times where you run, there are times where you walk, and there are times where you crawl. We call this a journey of life –adventurous journey of faith with highs and lows. This minute you are hot, this minute you are cold. The perfect example of this, is Elijah the man of God.

After showdown at mount Carmel with the prophets of Baal and Ashtoreth, after the victory in the land, the man of God Elijah was on the run for his life from the threats of Jezebel. You would expect the faith of Elijah to erupt overseeing the mighty hand of God by raining the fire down and raining it down after 3 years. But he listened to the wrong voice. Throughout the bible, this is the man who mastered the art of listening to the voice of God.

We also have our season as the body of Christ of lukewarm tendencies. In the words of Apostle Paul "Awake from your sleep". There are millions of voices of distraction but only one master's voice that can lead you into the right path. In nature, we are prophetic individual, it is of utmost important to discern the voice of the Lord out of millions of voices.

Incline your ear, you shall see the wonders of the Lord. We see calamity I our lives merely because we miss the voice of the Lord. Prophet Isaiah goes on further to say that "If you be obedient, you shall eat the good of the land". Obedience start by listening to the voice of God. You cannot obey what you haven't heard. Faith comes by hearing. You eventually mature in your spiritual walk with God when you keep on hearing His small still voice.

The meaning rest in the Lord, is to entirely leave everything under the hands of God. Your trust, your job, your marriage, your children, your health, and your finances under the umbrella of God.

Psalm 20:7 Some trust in chariots, and some in horses: but we will remember the
name of the LORD our God.

While some people trust in their own strength, money, power, or fame, we trust in the excellent name of the Lord. The name of the Lord is our refuge in times of trouble. In good times, in bad times, we shall lift up the praises of our mouth unto the glory of God. When we behold His face, we are not coming out with nothing but with the countenance of the Living God upon our faces.

Psalm 34:5 They looked unto him, and were lightened: and their faces were not
ashamed.

We look unto Christ the hope of our glory, and we shall never be ashamed. Christ is a conqueror and a victor. He is the great lion from the tribe of Judah. When we look unto Him, we become bold like lion. In this trying times, with a lot of things to question, rest in the Lord. Sometimes in your life, things do not make sense, you will find yourself trying to make sense of the spiritual things from a carnal mind, your intelligence find it hard comprehend the ways of the Lord.

It is high time we leave all unto the hands of the Lord. Rest, you shall be assured of your destiny. There is so many cities to conqueror, there is many hills to climb, the journey is still ahead. There are moment when you be like Elijah under the tree saying "I am no better than my ancestors, Lord take me". Take heart, the journey is still ahead. Rest in the Lord!

All things work together.

1. Romans 8:28 - "And we know that all things work together for good to them that love God, to them who are the called according to his purpose."

This scripture has kept me in tacked in many instances whereby I was going through the most. I will hear small whisper in ears "All things work together for good to those that love God". This is the whisper of the Holy spirit. the spirit within us bear witness to the Word of God and point us to Christ. Any spirit that does not point you to Christ is not of God. Even the mighty Angels of God when they come to you they will bear witness of Christ. We the body of Christ, our greatest commission is also to be witness of Jesus Christ.

The first man who bear witness of Christ is John the Baptist. Like John, we must point Christ where there is no life. Where there is no spirit of Christ, there is no peace. Therefore, there is no life. The spirit of Christ is the power of life itself.

When you are in Christ all things fall into places. Where there is no way, suddenly there is a way. Rocks can even gush out water for you. Rivers can flow even in the deserted place for you to drink. Christ is the way maker. Christ is in God. We are in Christ. And we are one with the Godhead. We are the sons and daughters of the Most High God through the power of the blood covenant of Christ. This is the love of God for humanity. God loved the whole world and so the need to deliverer a savior for us.

When times are getting hard, just know that God got it all under control. Be still in the Lord and rest in His unequivocal promises. The promises of God bring healing unto the land. Promises of God are blessings beyond blessings. Abraham was promised blessings 4000 year ago. Here we are still reaping the benefits of Abraham. What God has promised you will at any day expire. While you still in the land of the living, you shall see the glory of God upon your life. He who promises has a track record of faithfulness. This is the Mighty God of the universe.

Therefore, all things will work together when you are in Christ. In Christ is in the very presence of the love of God. Be hopeful. Be strong. Keep the fire of your faith burning in your heart.

Prayer and supplication.

1. *Philippians 4:6-7 - "Be careful for nothing; but in every thing by prayer and supplication with thanksgiving let your requests be made known unto God. And the peace of God, which passeth all understanding, shall keep your hearts and minds through Christ Jesus."*

I like this scripture when saying "In everything". This literally means in every aspect of your life, communicate with God. He will come through for you by giving you spiritual wisdom, knowledge and understanding. You need revelation from God to do mighty thing in your life. King Solomon was blessed beyond measure through his God given wisdom.

Wisdom will open doors for you, keep you, protect you, and honors you. When you pray, do shy away from asking a God given wisdom to look at things from God perspective. With your own eyes, challenges will seem like mount Everest, but with the eyes of the spirit, every challenge is an opportunity.

We all know about the power and the importance of prayer. Especially in dare times, prayer will keep you strong.

James 5:13 Is any among you afflicted? let him pray. Is any merry? let him sing
psalms.
14 Is any sick among you? let him call for the elders of the church; and let
them pray over him, anointing him with oil in the name of the Lord:

15 And the prayer of faith shall save the sick, and the Lord shall raise him
up; and if he have committed sins, they shall be forgiven him.

We are in the age where death is at the highest due to uncommon sicknesses and diseases. We are in the age where many things are rigged, food, media, education, health care etc. diseases are manufactured. Food are manufactured with evil intentions. Technology, robots and AIs are replacing human intelligence. With all these, we can stay above the system through the power of prayer. Man of God like Elijah, were controlled by the heavenly government, which is non-man-made.

Spirituality should be above every need. It is from your intimacy and relationship with God that you able to amount to something bigger than life. Let God backs you up. With many following the devil, stay with the team that would never loss—Team Jesus!

Pray, praise, worship, fast, and meditate on the Word of God. Pray with all kinds of prayer you shall see the sun arises with its arrays of healing wings. Your land shall be restored, and your seeds shall look lively. In God we trust. In God we boast all day long. Let the high praise be in thy lips from this day forward and forever more. Take care!

1. *John 14:27 - "Peace I leave with you, my peace I give unto you: not as the world giveth, give I unto you. Let not your heart be troubled, neither let it be afraid."*

When trouble mount up, we become peace less. We ponder each night, toss and turn, thinking about the predicament we are in. it is normal for human being to act like this. But as the sons of God with power, we know that God got everything under control. Rest in His promises and comfort your heart with scriptures of hope. With God, where there is no hope there is a hope. With God, where there is no way, there is a way. The Creator of the universe is active and alive in our lives. We do not serve a distant God.

He is within us. He is upon us. His eyes are upon the nations. He is high above the nation. It is He who sit above the circle of the earth. This is the God who made convent with Abraham who still make his presence known even to this day and age.

He is the God of peace. When you are still, you shall know that He is God. His holy spirit within you shall comfort your soul. It is His work to keep you in the joy of the Lord. To help you grow and mature in spiritual things in the Lord—and to know and experience the power of salvation. For salvation comes only from the Lord God through the name of Jesus Christ.

The greatest blessing God can give is His peace. Not just peace but abundant peace that comes flowing from His throne of light. The peace of the Lord God will keep you steady even in difficult times. Even when war can arise, you shall be calm and collected.

The peace of the Lord is different from the peace you can get in this world. Money can only guarantee you a certain security but will not grant you peace. Money can only give you choice and freedom of what you want but not what you need.

God gives you what you need and what you do not know that you need. The spirit of God searches hearts of men and knows the will of God and what you need the most. This is the greatest gift to the mankind especially those who see the need of a savior in their life. The truth is that, not all people see the need to have Jesus in their life. The absence of the Holy Spirit in your life is the absence of Christ. Where there is the spirit of God, there is liberty. Only the truth shall set you free. And the truth of Christ brings you peace. Allow the peace of Crist to rule your heart. Issues of this life will bring you down, only the God of peace can lift you up. God bless!

God wants to prosper you.

1. *Jeremiah 29:11 - "For I know the thoughts that I think toward you, saith the Lord, thoughts of peace, and not of evil, to give you an expected end."*

God knows the end from the beginning. He is the master of the destiny of men and women. His love and favor are towards the children of men. His mighty hand of righteousness gives us victory all the time. We can do so much in the kingdom business through the grace and mercy of God. It is not by might of men and women but is by the mighty spirit of God that works righteousness in all.

This is the spirit of humility that we must work in. as I always say, humility is a way to the heart of God. King Ahab of Israel went soft before the Lord after he committed countless of evil act, the act was enough to move the heart of God—and that act was humility. Humble yourself, God shall lift you up. God shall restore you and heal your wounds.

The countenance of the Lord God shines upon you. The thoughts of God towards you are for peace and prosperity. Prosperity of God includes all facet of life, spiritually, mentally, materially and physically. God blessed Solomon with spiritual wisdom, and all the wealth came after that. It is a disaster to have wealth while you are spiritually immature. You will lose it all. You have to know God and His ways.

Brethren, be planted in the house of God. You will save yourself from all the trouble, and all the temptation that easily entangle us. The Word of God will deepen your faith in God and you will have a deeper experience of God and stand in times of trouble. Stand is an unequivocal authority and faith in the Lord.

We all have dreams and visions for our lives but it God who shall bring an expected end. Trust the Lord with your career, education, finances, marriage and family, the Lord God through Christ never disappoint. Shame will be far from you. Blessings comes from the Lord. Joy and happiness in found in Jesus Christ. Being planted in the house of the Lord to have you run this race with strength and might from the Lord even during hard times. Trust in the salvation of God.

1. *Isaiah 40:31 - "But they that wait upon the Lord shall renew their strength; they shall mount up with wings as eagles; they shall run, and not be weary; and they shall walk, and not faint."*

You who wait upon the Lord, you shall renew your strength. The Word of the Lord in a season, can deliver you from ancient evil stronghold that have been tampering with your ancestors. Most of the time we talk about the power of the Word but never teach believers how to hear the voice of God. You will ten times ahead of your brethren if you can discern the voice of the Holy Spirit.

The understanding and wisdom that Daniel prayed for is vital if you are to walk in spirit and be able to discern. Spirit of discernment is also part of the 9 gifts of spirits. We do not only deal with good spirits but also with bad ones. it's a total lie that believers encounters angels only; we encounter both world.

As a prophetic individual you are likely to do spiritual warfare most of the time as you are contending with the kingdom of darkness. If you are ignorant of the devices of the enemy, you are likely to face defeat. But the righteous may fall many times, but the Lord always raise the up.

The tribe of Issachar had spiritual understanding of the time and seasons. Waiting in the Lord means you are waiting to hear the sweet voice of the Holy spirit for your next move. It means you will have to move when God moves. Just like the man of God Elijah, he had a special ability of discerning spirits. Same as Elisha, who sometimes tapped into music for prophetic inspiration.

This comes after spending time with the Lord in the secret place, studying and meditating in the Word. Also not neglecting the principle of prayer and fasting. Apostles and prophets after Jesus ascended to heaven, could not take great decision without applying the element of fasting in their prayer life.

I have written a lot about the power of prayer and fasting, it is the powerhouse of prayer. Some stronghold of evil without fasting cannot leave. If you are someone who is constantly spiritually attacked, this is the perfect remedy.

Mathews 17:21 Howbeit this kind goeth not out but by prayer and fasting.

We pray with all kinds of prayer while waiting in the Lord.

The Lord is my light.

1. Psalm 27:1 - "The Lord is my light and my salvation; whom shall I fear? the Lord is the strength of my life; of whom shall I be afraid?"

In the beginning, God said "Let there be light". The earth needed light, and we need light. Where there is light, there is wisdom, knowledge and understanding. Where there is light, vision stand. Darkness is the absence of light. God made light, and divided light from the darkness. First and foremost, He did not create darkness. Darkness was already there.

The statement "Let there be light" is not a light one, in light there is life and everything that you will ever need. From speaking about the light, we are not talking about the arrays of the sun. we are talking about the presence of God. We talking about God extending His essence to our planet. Jesus Christ came in this world as the light. He descended from the unapproachable light of God, the light that Enoch saw.

I also believe that the first man on this earth, Adam. Also saw the glimpse of the future redemption. As the first Adam, I also believe that he saw the second Adam long ago, the man who was to restore man and women back to the Garden. In the Garden of Eden, they had a special relationship with their maker. This Holy spirit that we are talking about, that indwells us, it is this that will help us return to the Garden, to presence of the Living God.

• • • •

WE ARE THE CHILDREN of Zion. Isaiah wrote "*Let us walk in the light of God*". Brethren, we need the light of God. David was not just making up words when He said "The Lord is my light and my salvation". He knew that light of God would lead him into the salvation of God. Into the rest of God.

Isaiah 43:10 Ye are my witnesses, saith the LORD, and my servant whom I have
chosen: that ye may know and believe me, and understand that I am he: before
me there was no God formed, neither shall there be after me.

John the Baptist came to be he witness of the Light. And that light gave the believers the power to be the sons of God. We are also the light of this world through Christ. As Christ is he, so are we in this world.

The light is also the truth of God. Thus the righteous are to walk in spirit and truth. He said "I am the way, the truth, and the life". Truth is part of his personality. Truth is who He is. And life is the light of the glory of God, for His spirit sustains the sons of men.

Believer, as you are the light of the world, wear the garment of truth. The garment of truth is your shield against the wiles of the enemy. The devil is called the fathers of all lies. In his there is truth, if you happen to be the truth, you have triumph, for he is a liar of all liars. If there was truth in the world, the world would have been Eden. Hang on unto the garment of Christ for your salvation, believe in him, you shall not be ashamed even in ages to come. Hallelujah!

1. *2 Corinthians 1:3-4 - "Blessed be God, even the Father of our Lord Jesus Christ, the Father of mercies, and the God of all comfort; Who comforteth us in all our tribulation, that we may be able to comfort them which are in any trouble, by the comfort wherewith we ourselves are comforted of God."*

In this end times, the spirit of comfort is at work. When your soul is drained, you need the restorer of soul. Believers who are sons of encouragement like Barnabas may encourage and comfort but the highest level of comfort is when the spirit of reaches you personally and speak comfort to your soul. The call of God is not a walk in part, it is a difficult task that need a heavenly back up since you are saving souls from damnation.

You soul need salvation too. Lie me, if you are into the Word of God daily, your spirit will put scripture in remembrance in times of need. And the relevant scripture will pop up. I comfort myself with scripture. I see Christ in light of scripture besides personal revelation, dreams and visions. Being grounded in scripture will keep you going, it is food for the soul.

David as the shepherd of the sheep, will revive the sheep's when they are tired or in need of food or water. Like us, as the sheep of the Most High God, there a times where we need to hear his small still voice in a unique way for comfort. All the greatest prophets, at some point in their lives felt lonely, worthless, defeated and depressed. Some even contested to God to take back his gift. Some even went on to run away from their calling like Jonah. Some even desired death.

It is beautiful adventurous journey of faith. Even Christ Himself felt rejected, lonely, and unwelcomed. It is the small still voice of the mighty God that will sustain you and steady fast you in your faith and stand.

Cheer up! He is the Father of mercy, and the God of comfort. He is willing and able to comfort us when we are in tribulations. It is the aspect of the Holy Spirit that is within us that bear witness to our trials and tribulations, and it is His role to comfort us with peace. He is the God of abundance peace. He shall fill you up with his blessing of peace. Totally, it is a blessing to live in peace amidst trials.

Isaiah 40:1-2Comfort ye, comfort ye my people, saith your God.
2 Speak ye comfortably to Jerusalem, and cry unto her, that her warfare is
accomplished, that her iniquity is pardoned: for she hath received of the LORD's
hand double for all her sins.

When you read the book of Isaiah, you will notice that its start with judgement over nations, as you read along from chapter 40 to the last chapter it's all about comfort and restoration. He is the comforter of souls. Be comforted in the Lord. Allow the Holy Spirit of God to work in your life. Desire spiritual gifts, especially prophetic gifts that your spiritual eyes can see beyond what your physical eyes can see. I wish all believers to walk in the spirit of prophecy as prophecy is for encouraging, comforting and exhorting. It is the spirit of prophecy that does that.

*I Corinthians 14:1-3 Follow after charity, and desire spiritual
gifts, but rather that ye may
prophesy.
2 For he that speaketh in an unknown tongue speaketh not unto
men, but
unto God: for no man understandeth him; howbeit in the spirit he
speaketh
mysteries.
3 But he that prophesieth speaketh unto men to edification, and
exhortation,
and comfort.*

Seek the righteousness of God.

1. Matthew 6:33 - "But seek ye first the kingdom of God, and his righteousness; and all these things shall be added unto you."

Usually believers who seek God for what He can do for them not what they can do for God, they don't last. We see brother and sister who has long ago forgotten about their faith because they did not get jobs, marriages, promotions, business opportunities, leadership roles within churches, financial breakthroughs etc. the preaching and teaching of this age, has equated faith with material gain. It's like when you don't have a car to drive to church, your faith is weak, your faith is this and that.

This is wide spread prosperity sermons that has weaken some of brother's spirit for not gaining, as they see it fit, according to their faith. Don't get me wrong, God is the God of all things. Psalm 24 says the whole earth and everything in it belong to God. Seek first the kingdom of God and all things shall be added unto you. God can bless you with abundance of peace. God can bless you with joy in spirit. God can bless you with long satisfying age. God can bless you with billions. God can bless you with blessings your room cannot contain. But at the e end of the day, it all comes to this "Seek the kingdom and His righteousness".

It is the kingdom that has whatsoever than you need. It is written that you are the ambassadors of Christ, it means you are the ambassadors of the kingdom of heaven while on earth. It means that through you the world must know Christ. Most of all, the world must know who you represent—and you represent all aspect of the kingdom, including blessings, honor and power. For you are the Sons of the Most High God you have exalted you through the cross of Jesus Christ. He has raised you up in Christ, seated in the heavenly places of authority in all things.

The kingdom of God is far greater, and has more in store than what our mere mind can comprehend. Men like Daniel and David sought the Lord with all their hearts regardless of their position within the society. Remember that, David had a huge responsibility as the King of Israel, however, he would not sleep until he sees the ark of the covenant in the temple. A man zealous for the kingdom business of God. God rewards those. Daniel made a choice not to eat the Babylonian food but rather went for a light diet of green food (Veggies). We saw the outcome of that, that he was able to discern the spiritual atmosphere of the heavenly things. He was granted special ability to interpret dreams and vision by the mighty spirit of God. He paid the sacrifice of a fasted and prayer life. He became the great men of understanding, wisdom and knowledge through the grace of God. It is all grace, folks.

You can do the same, by sacrificing your flesh. Every day we have to die to ourselves for spirit of Christ to move in our lives. Holiness is power. Holiness will get you in places where men and women will never set their feet in. and the beautiful thing about it is that, it comes through faith. While faith comes through heart believing the Word of God. Holiness, faith and righteousness will keep you—and eventually will honor you. Let Christ reigns in your heart.

1. Psalm 46:1 - "God is our refuge and strength, a very present help in trouble."

I have lived with this psalm verse for so many years. And I understand that a refuge is a place of safety. For we are stranger in this planet called earth. Any time can be your day to go home. While we still under the sun, lets live every minute of it for Christ. See Christ every day, and you will make everybody's day.

You do not only need a refuge but also a strength. And God is both and more. The God of the universe will keep you, protect you, guide and bless you in due season. There are times a season for everything. Keep your soul free from the issues of this life. Meaning, press on to what is good and neglect what can deter you from your faith. Paul also talk about foolish talks, Neglect those. Keep the focus.

A very presence help in times of trouble" mean that trouble bound to be there. But my God and your God will be there when all hell broke. God is never early or too late. Same applies to your breakthrough. Our God is the God of breakthroughs. Even when people look down on you, or hoped that you never amount to anything, God will raise the standard in your life. Your life shall be a new testament in your village, or town, that God liveth. The Holy One of Israel is till the God of this world.

It is faith that pleases Him. A simple faith can move mountains. The bible says that as small as mustard seed, faith can move mountains. We have a hall of fame of faith in Hebrews

11. Even prostitute saw the kingdom of God through faith. They were honored and raised up because of they faith. Faith is power. Faith is an action, or the footsteps of righteous believers who walk the walk, and talk the talk of victory.

The power is in your mouth. Speak the talk of faith. Speak victory. Already you have the promises of God laid out in the bible. Keep proclaiming and confessing those scriptures. The arrays of light of God shall come. You shall succeed.

1. Romans 15:13 - "Now the God of hope fill you with all joy and peace in believing, that ye may abound in hope, through the power of the Holy Ghost."

The God of hope with fill your heart with sweet words as honey when you are going through the most. Going through the most is when all thing are going south instead of up north. We all want success and to progress in life.

Psalm 27:13 I had fainted, unless I had believed to see the goodness of the LORD in
the land of the living.

If it was the hope that David had in the Lord, he would have long ago fainted. This is even true to some of us, when thing are getting tougher, worse and worse, and on top of that you are believing God for your breakthrough, many end up leaving their faith. If it is not a tested faith, it is not enough to carry you through the storms.

The saint's faith was tested. Test is part of life. The perfect example of this is Abraham. We all know the story of Abraham. What kept Abraham going is the personal revelations he had about the mighty God, whom he called Almighty God. After meeting with Melchizedek, he started calling him Most High God.

Through his walk with God, he had revelation after revelation about the person of God. We also have to mature in spirit to be able to stand test and the wiles of the enemy. The story of Abraham is a life of hope, not just hope but unshakable hope in the name of the Lord. He pressed on till he received the promises of God. He is still blessing the Most High even today for seeing his promises being fulfilled upon earth.

Through Abraham the world is blessed. Through the seed of Abraham, the world is one with God for those who believe as Abraham did. Abraham believed God, and it was counted to him as righteousness. Abraham was before the law, however, pleased the Lord through his faith walk. The walk that Enoch walked.

The weapon of the end time to overcome our adversities is faith, hope and love. You cannot have one and not have the other. I remember at one point in my life going through difficult and hard time that lead me into depression, during that season, I had a personal revelation of the faith of Abraham, in a vision of the night, he told me that the just shall live by faith. Even to this day, when I'm going south—sinking in faith, or in a situation that feels hopeless, I can still hear this words "The just shall live by faith".

This is a message from me to you "The just shall live by faith". Christ was pleased by faith. He walked in faith, and taught in faith. Faith is the power walk of God. Faith and obedience walks together like brothers. Faith is the hope in the unseen. Hope is part of the game here. Hope in the Lord. It is faith that overcomes the world.

The righteous shall not be moved.

1. *Psalm 55:22 - "Cast thy burden upon the Lord, and he shall sustain thee: he shall never suffer the righteous to be moved."*

The refuge of the righteous is the Lord Himself. He shields them like a hen over its young ones. Under the wings of the Almighty God they shall rest in hope and abound in peace. Cast your burden unto the Lord, you shall rest in the Lord. As Joshua allocated thee tribes land, in the Lord your soul and your spirit shall rest abundantly.

He shall sustain you with His strength. His love shall be your assurance. His Holy spirit reach you even in the night times. You shall hear the small still voice of the Holy spirit guiding you, assuring you and comforting you. Be comforted in the name of the Lord. This is the difficult season were are in, that if the Word of God is not build up in you, you will be dismayed.

Deuteronomy 31:6 - "Be strong and of a good courage, fear not, nor be afraid of them: for the Lord thy God, he it is that doth go with thee; he will not fail thee, nor forsake thee."

Moses strengthened the nation of Israel with this words. Joshua was also strengthened with this words "Be strong and courageous". Even when the heavenly host meet with you, whether in dreams or vision, they will say to you "Do not be afraid". The driving force of any man or women is courage. The righteous are bold as lion.

There must come a time in your life where you just want to totally depend in the strength of the Lord. Every one of us have faith, it just need to be stirred up. And through faith teaching, you can start seeing wonders in your life if you can practice what faith teaches. Healing, miracles and great deliverance shall be your second nature. Meaning, shall be normal.

Let us cast all our burden unto the Lord. He cares for you, He loves us, He has redeemed us, and highly anointed us for times like this. Let the banner of the name of the Lord fly high. Let all the nation see the excellency of the Lord. The Lord God is great at all times. Even during critical times, lets worship, praise and thank the Holy One of Israel. For it is by grace that all of us are still in the land of the living. There are times where you could have been out completely, but the Lord of Host came through for you with His mighty angels to rescue you.

Personally, if it was not the Lord, I would have been long dead by now. The enemy would have destroyed me

1. *John 16:33 - "These things I have spoken unto you, that in me ye might have peace. In the world ye shall have tribulation: but be of good cheer; I have overcome the world."*

In tough times, when life throws its hardest punches and you feel like you're being tossed around in a stormy sea, remember this: you're not alone. Even though the road ahead might seem dark and uncertain, there's a light that shines brighter than any darkness. That light is the hope we find in the Lord.

Let's be real. Life isn't always easy. There are moments when it feels like everything is falling apart, when challenges come crashing down like waves, threatening to overwhelm us. But here's the thing: we were never promised a life free of trials. In fact, in John 16:33, it says, "In the world ye shall have tribulation." So, yes, hard times will come. But that's not where the story ends. The story end in victory. The story end when your banner is lift up for all to see the wonders of the God of Mount Zion!

The beauty lies in what comes next: "but be of good cheer; I have overcome the world." These words, spoken by Jesus himself, are like a beacon of hope shining through the storm clouds. They remind us that no matter how tough things get, we have a reason to keep going. We have a reason to hold on to hope. Christ himself held unto hope till the Cross. He is our perfect example since He was tempted in all things but overcame.

The same God who created the universe, the same God who parted the Red Sea, the same God who conquered death itself – He's on your side. He's fighting for you. And if He's for you, who can be against you? No one really.

So, my friend, when the going gets tough, don't lose heart. Don't let fear and doubt creep in. Instead, hang unto the promises of God. Remember that He's with you every step of the way, guiding you, strengthening you, and lifting you up when you feel like you can't go on.

It's okay to feel overwhelmed. It's okay to cry out in frustration. But don't stay there. Lift your eyes to the heavens and remind yourself of the truth: you are loved, you are valued, and you are never alone. Above all, that you have a Father that has given you the kingdom as the inheritance for now and the age to come in Christ.

And here's the best part: the story doesn't end with the trials and tribulations. No, there's a glorious ending waiting for those who put their trust in the Lord. A future filled with hope, joy, and peace beyond all understanding.

Hold on to that hope. Keep your eyes fixed on Jesus, the author and perfecter of your faith. And when the storms rage, be of good cheer, for He has overcome the world.

You've got this. And more importantly, He's got you. So keep pressing on, keep believing, and keep shining your light in the darkness. Your best days are still ahead, and with God by your side, nothing is impossible.

He cares about you.

1. 1 Peter 5:7 - "Casting all your care upon him; for he careth for you."

In the midst of life's chaos and uncertainty, it's easy to feel overwhelmed by worry and anxiety. The good news is that you don't have to carry that burden alone. You have a loving Father who cares about you more than you can imagine.

In 1 Peter 5:7, it says, *"Casting all your care upon him; for he careth for you."* These words are like a gentle reminder from a friend, urging you to let go of your worries and place your trust in God's loving hands. He doesn't want you to bear the weight of your concerns on your own shoulders. He wants to carry them for you.

The same God who knows every star by name, the same God who knit you together in your mother's womb, He cares about the smallest details of your life. He knows your fears, your struggles, and your pain, and He longs to bring you comfort and peace. As always, He think good thoughts towards you. He will give you power in times of need. The kingdom of God is the kingdom of grace and mercy. Mercy and grace abounds more.

Brethren, when life feels overwhelming and the weight of your worries threatens to crush you, remember that you are not alone. You have a heavenly Father who is always there for you, ready to listen, ready to comfort, ready to provide for your every need. It is also written *"I can do all things through Christ who strengthens me"*.

That doesn't mean that life will always be easy. There will still be challenges to face and obstacles to overcome. But you can face them with confidence, knowing that God is on your side. He's fighting for you, He's working all things together for your good, and He will never leave you nor forsake you.

Hence, don't be afraid to cast your cares upon Him. Lay down your burdens at His feet and trust that He will carry you through. He's not just a distant, aloof God; He's a loving Father who cares about every aspect of your life.

And as you release your worries and fears into His capable hands, you'll experience a peace that surpasses all understanding. A peace that calms the storm raging within your soul and fills you with hope and confidence for the future.

So, my dear friend, take heart. You are deeply loved, you are cherished, and you are never alone. And with God by your side, you can face whatever comes your way with courage and grace.

Through prayer in the name of the Lord we shall do valiant things.

I will be with you.

1. *Isaiah 43:2 - "When thou passest through the waters, I will be with thee; and through the rivers, they shall not overflow thee: when thou walkest through the fire, thou shalt not be burned; neither shall the flame kindle upon thee."*

Imagine walking through deep waters or facing a raging fire. It's a terrifying thought, isn't it? But here's the incredible promise that God offers us: He will be with us every step of the way. He doesn't promise to remove the waters or extinguish the flames, but He does promise to walk beside us, to guide us, and to protect us from harm.

When life's challenges threaten to overwhelm us, when it feels like we're drowning in despair or being consumed by the flames of adversity, God is there. He's not watching from a distance, waiting for us to figure it out on our own. No, He's right there with us, holding our hand, whispering words of comfort and strength.

Just think about it. The same God who calmed the stormy seas with a word, the same God who rescued Daniel from the lion's den, He's walking beside you, ready to lead you through the darkest valleys and the fiercest fires.

Take courage. You are not alone in this journey. You have a faithful God who has promised to never leave you nor forsake you. He will be with you through the waters, through the rivers, through the fires, and He will ensure that you emerge unscathed on the other side.

That doesn't mean that life will always be easy. There will still be trials and tribulations to face. But you can face them with confidence, knowing that the God of the universe is on your side.

So, when you find yourself in the midst of life's storms, when the waters rise and the flames threaten to engulf you, remember this promise: "I will be with you." Let those words sink deep into your soul and fill you with hope and courage.

And as you journey through life's ups and downs, may you always remember that you are never alone. God is with you, guiding you, protecting you, and loving you every step of the way. So, fear not, my friend, for He is faithful, and He will see you through to victory

He doesn't promise to shield us from life's trials, nor does He promise that we won't feel the heat of the flames or the pull of the currents. Instead, He promises His presence, His guidance, and His protection.

Just as He was with Moses as he led the Israelites through the parted Red Sea, just as He was with Shadrach, Meshach, and Abednego in the fiery furnace, He is with us in our trials today. He walks beside us, His hand steady and His voice calming our fears.

As you journey through life's storms, may you find strength in His presence, peace in His promises, and hope in His unfailing love. For He is the God who walks on water, the God who quenches the flames, and the God who holds you in the palm of His hand.

So, fear not, my friend. Whatever challenges may come your way, remember this: He is with you, and He will see you through.

My Help comes from the Lord.

Psalm 121:1-2 - "I will lift up mine eyes unto the hills, from whence cometh my help. My help cometh from the Lord, which made heaven and earth."

Imagine standing at the foot of a towering mountain, gazing up at its majestic peaks. In that moment, it's easy to feel small and insignificant, overwhelmed by the vastness of the world around you. But in that same moment, there's a profound truth that resonates deep within your soul: your help comes from the Lord.

The psalmist understood this truth intimately. As he looked up at the hills, he didn't see them as insurmountable obstacles. Instead, he saw them as a reminder of the greatness of God, the one who made heaven and earth. And in that recognition, he found hope and reassurance.

You see, the God who created the mountains, the God who set the stars in the sky, He is the same God who watches over you and cares for you. He is your ever-present help in times of trouble, your steadfast anchor in the midst of life's storms.

When you find yourself facing challenges that seem too big to overcome, lift up your eyes to the hills. Remember that your help comes from the Lord, the maker of heaven and earth. He is more powerful than any mountain you may face, more steadfast than any obstacle in your path.

And as you place your trust in Him, you'll find that He is faithful to sustain you, to strengthen you, and to guide you through every trial and tribulation. His love for you knows no bounds, and His grace is more than sufficient for all your needs.

Lift up your eyes, my friend, and fix your gaze on the one who holds the universe in His hands. For in Him, you will find the strength, the courage, and the hope to face whatever lies ahead.

Cheer up!

The Lord delivers me.

Psalm 34:19 - "Many are the afflictions of the righteous: but the Lord delivereth him out of them all."

L ife is full of challenges, and no one is immune to difficulties. Even those who strive to live righteously face their fair share of afflictions. But here's the comforting truth: the Lord is faithful to deliver His people out of every trial they encounter.

It's important to recognize that being righteous doesn't mean we won't face hardships. In fact, the Bible acknowledges that afflictions are a common experience for believers. However, what sets us apart is our hope and confidence in the Lord's deliverance.

When we find ourselves in the midst of trials—whether they be physical, emotional, or spiritual—we can take comfort in knowing that we serve a God who is greater than any challenge we face. He is our refuge and our strength, a present help in times of trouble.

No matter how overwhelming our afflictions may seem, we can trust that the Lord is working behind the scenes, orchestrating our deliverance. He has promised to never leave us nor forsake us, and He is faithful to keep His word.

So, my friend, if you find yourself weighed down by the burdens of life, take heart. You are not alone in your struggles. The Lord is with you, ready to lift you up and carry you through. He is your ever-present help, your shield and your fortress.

And as you place your trust in Him, you can rest assured that He will deliver you out of every affliction you face. His love for you knows no bounds, and His power is more than sufficient to overcome any obstacle in your path.

So, cling to the promise of Psalm 34:19. Let it be a source of strength and encouragement as you navigate life's ups and downs. And remember, no matter how many afflictions may come your way, the Lord is faithful to deliver you out of them all.

He shall supply all my needs.

Philippians 4:19 - "But my God shall supply all your need according to his riches in glory by Christ Jesus."

The riches and glory of God are in Christ. Christ offered masses healing and deliverance in His ministry. With God nothing is impossible, He is standing in the right hand of God interceding for us in all things. There is nothing wrong being wealthy, healthy and blessed abundantly materially.

The principle is that you do not have to put all your heart into money making. The righteous are blessed even when asleep. Look unto God, and He shall look out for you like He did for Job. Job was blessed beyond measure. Solomon was wealthy too. Abraham was blessed in all aspects. The blessings of God add no sorrow in your life. And they come with honor, glory and power.

In a world that often feels marked by scarcity and insufficiency, these words offer a beacon of hope *""But my God shall supply all your need according to his riches in glory by Christ Jesus."*

They remind us that we serve a God who is not limited by earthly constraints, but who is able to provide for all our needs abundantly.

It's easy to become consumed by worry and anxiety when we're faced with financial struggles, health concerns, or other challenges. But in Philippians 4:19, we're reminded that our God is a generous provider who cares deeply about our well-being.

He doesn't promise to give us everything we want, but He does promise to meet our needs according to His glorious riches.

And His riches are limitless, far surpassing anything we could ever imagine.

if you find yourself in a season of need, take heart. You serve a God who sees your circumstances and who is more than able to meet you where you are. He knows what you need before you even ask, and He delights in providing for His children.

Trust in His provision, knowing that He is faithful to fulfill His promises. And as you lean on Him in faith, you'll discover that His provision exceeds your expectations and brings glory to His name.

And as you rest in His provision, may you experience the peace that surpasses all understanding, knowing that your God shall supply all your need according to His riches in glory by Christ Jesus.

Psalm 91:1-2 - "He that dwelleth in the secret place of the most High shall abide under the shadow of the Almighty. I will say of the Lord, He is my refuge and my fortress: my God; in him will I trust."

I magine yourself in the secret place of the Most High, hidden away from the storms and chaos of this world, safely sheltered under the shadow of the Almighty. In this sacred space, you find refuge and strength, knowing that you are under the watchful care of your Heavenly Father.

You can tap into this place through the grace of the Holy Spirit. because now we have boldness to enter into throne room of grace and mercy. You can be the resident of this place because Christ has paid the price. The landlord of this place is the Almighty God. He is your refuge. Faith, holiness, righteousness and His grace will keep you. Believe in the goodness of the Lord. Taste His goodness.

The psalmist declares with confidence, *"He is my refuge and my fortress: my God; in him will I trust."* These words are a powerful declaration of faith, a bold affirmation of the psalmist's unwavering confidence in God's ability to protect and provide.

God is not only our refuge and fortress; He is also our ever-present help in times of need. He is our strength when we are weak, our comforter when we are distressed, and our protector when we are in danger.

So, my friend, if you find yourself facing challenges or feeling anxious about the future, take refuge in the Lord. Rest in His presence, knowing that He is with you always, guiding you, protecting you, and leading you in the way you should go.

Declare with confidence, *"He is my refuge and my fortress: my God; in him will I trust."* And as you place your trust in Him, may you experience His peace and His presence in abundance, knowing that you are safe and secure under the shadow of the Almighty.

I Can do all things.

Philippians 4:13 - "I can do all things through Christ which strengtheneth me."

These words serve as a powerful reminder of the limitless strength and empowerment that believers have access to through their relationship with Christ. In a world filled with challenges, obstacles, and uncertainties, this verse offers hope, encouragement, and a renewed sense of purpose.

When we read *"I can do all things,"* it's important to understand that this doesn't mean we can achieve anything on our own strength or abilities. Rather, it's an acknowledgment of our dependency on Christ and His empowering presence in our lives. Through Him, we gain the strength, wisdom, and courage to face whatever challenges come our way.

Life often presents us with trials that seem insurmountable, dreams that appear out of reach, and tasks that feel overwhelming. In those moments, it's easy to feel discouraged or inadequate. But Philippians 4:13 reminds us that we are not alone in our struggles. We have a Savior who walks beside us, offering His strength and guidance every step of the way.

It's worth noting that the source of our strength is not found within ourselves or in our own abilities. Rather, it comes from our connection to Christ. He is the one who strengthens us, equips us, and enables us to accomplish His purposes in our lives.

This verse is not a promise of success in every endeavor or a guarantee of a trouble-free life. Rather, it's an invitation to trust in Christ's sufficiency and rely on His power to see us through every circumstance. Whether we're facing adversity, pursuing our dreams, or simply navigating the ups and downs of daily life, we can do so with confidence, knowing that Christ is with us, strengthening us, and empowering us to overcome.

As believers, our faith in Christ transforms our perspective on challenges. Instead of seeing obstacles as barriers to our success, we view them as opportunities for God to demonstrate His power and faithfulness in our lives. In moments of weakness, we find strength in His presence. In times of doubt, we find reassurance in His promises. And in times of despair, we find hope in His unfailing love.

Ultimately, Philippians 4:13 is a declaration of faith—a declaration that we are more than conquerors through Christ who strengthens us. It's a reminder that no matter what we face, we can trust in His ability to see us through. So let us embrace this truth, lean into His strength, and live each day with confidence, knowing that with Christ, we truly can do all things.

With all the saying, keep declaring your faith in God. There is power in your testimony. And that testimony comes from your mouth. The power of life and death is in your tongue. Be comforted in the name of Jesus Christ.

Psalm Scripture of Comfort from 1-150.

But thou, O LORD, art a shield for me; my glory, and the lifter
up of mine head.
Psalm:3:3
I will both lay me down in peace, and sleep: for thou, LORD,
only makest me dwell in safety.
Psalm:4:8
For thou, LORD, wilt bless the righteous; with favour wilt thou
compass him as with a shield.
Psalm:5:12
Out of the mouth of babes and sucklings hast thou ordained
strength because of thine enemies, that thou mightest still the
enemy and the avenger.
Psalm:8:2
For thou hast made him a little lower than the angels, and hast
crowned him with glory and honour.
Psalm:8:5
The LORD also will be a refuge for the oppressed, a refuge in
times of trouble.
Psalm:9:9
The words of the LORD are pure words: as silver tried in a
furnace of earth, purified seven times.
Psalm:12:6
The LORD is the portion of mine inheritance and of my cup:
thou maintainest my lot.
Psalm:16:5
Hold up my goings in thy paths, that my footsteps slip not.

Psalm:17:5

Keep me as the apple of the eye, hide me under the shadow of
thy wings,

Psalm:17:8

As for me, I will behold thy face in Righteousness: I shall be
satisfied, when I awake, with thy likeness.

Psalm:17:15

The LORD is my rock, and my fortress, and my deliverer; my
God, my strength, in whom I will trust; my buckler, and the
horn of my salvation, and my high tower.

Psalm:18:2

I will call upon the LORD, who is worthy to be praised: so shall
I be saved from mine enemies.

Psalm:18:3

It is God that girdeth me with strength, and maketh my way
perfect.

Psalm:18:32

Great deliverance giveth he to his king; and sheweth mercy to
his anointed, to David, and to his seed for evermore.

Psalm:18:50

The law of the LORD is perfect, converting the soul: the
testimony of the LORD is sure, making wise the simple.

Psalm:19:7

Some trust in chariots, and some in horses: but we will
remember the name of the LORD our God.

Psalm:20:7

Be thou exalted, LORD, in thine own strength: so will we sing
and praise thy power.

Psalm:21:13

But thou art holy, O thou that inhabitest the praises of Israel.

Psalm:22:3
The LORD is my shepherd; I shall not want.
Psalm:23:1
Surely goodness and mercy shall follow me all the days of my
life: and I will dwell in the house of the LORD for ever.
Psalm:23:6
Who is this King of glory? The LORD strong and mighty, the
LORD mighty in battle.
Psalm:24:8
The secret of the LORD is with them that fear him; and he will
shew them his covenant.
Psalm:25:14
Mine eyes are ever toward the LORD; for he shall pluck my feet
out of the net.
Psalm:25:15
The LORD is my light and my salvation; whom shall I fear? the
LORD is the strength of my life; of whom shall I be afraid?
Psalm:27:1
I had fainted, unless I had believed to see the goodness of the
LORD in the land of the living.
Psalm:27:13

• • • •

The LORD is my strength and my shield; my heart trusted in
him, and I am helped: therefore my heart greatly rejoiceth; and
with my song will I praise him.
Psalm:28:7
For his anger endureth but a moment; in his favour is life:
weeping may endure for a night, but joy cometh in the morning.
Psalm:30:5

Be of good courage, and he shall strengthen your heart, all ye
that hope in the LORD.
Psalm:31:24
Thou art my hiding place; thou shalt preserve me from trouble;
thou shalt compass me about with songs of deliverance. Selah.
Psalm:32:7
By the word of the LORD were the heavens made; and all the
host of them by the breath of his mouth.
Psalm:33:6
For he spake, and it was done; he commanded, and it stood fast.
Psalm:33:9
I sought the LORD, and he heard me, and delivered me from
all my fears.
Psalm:34:4
They looked unto him, and were lightened: and their faces were
not ashamed.
Psalm:34:5
The angel of the LORD encampeth round about them that fear
him, and delivereth them.
Psalm:34:7
Let them shout for joy, and be glad, that favour my righteous
cause: yea, let them say continually, Let the LORD be
magnified, which hath pleasure in the prosperity of his servant.
Psalm:35:27
Thy righteousness is like the great mountains; thy judgments are
a great deep: O LORD, thou preservest man and beast.
Psalm:36:6
They shall be abundantly satisfied with the fatness of thy house;
and thou shalt make them drink of the river of thy pleasures.
Psalm:36:8

Delight thyself also in the LORD: and he shall give thee the desires of thine heart.
Psalm:37:4
Hear my prayer, O LORD, and give ear unto my cry; hold not thy peace at my tears: for I am a stranger with thee, and a sojourner, as all my fathers were.
Psalm:39:12
But I am poor and needy; yet the Lord thinketh upon me: thou art my help and my deliverer; make no tarrying, O my God.
Psalm:40:17
The LORD will strengthen him upon the bed of languishing: thou wilt make all his bed in his sickness.
Psalm:41:3
Blessed be the LORD God of Israel from everlasting, and to everlasting. Amen, and Amen.
Psalm:41:13
Why art thou cast down, O my soul? and why art thou disquieted within me? hope thou in God: for I shall yet praise him, who is the health of my countenance, and my God.
Psalm:42:11
O send out thy light and thy truth: let them lead me; let them bring me unto thy holy hill, and to thy tabernacles.
Psalm:43:3

. . . .

Through thee will we push down our enemies: through thy name will we tread them under that rise up against us.
Psalm:44:5
In God we boast all the day long, and praise thy name for ever. Selah.

Psalm:44:8
God is our refuge and strength, a very present help in trouble.
Psalm:46:1
He shall choose our inheritance for us, the excellency of Jacob
whom he loved. Selah.
Psalm:47:4
For this God is our God for ever and ever: he will be our guide
even unto death.
Psalm:48:14
But God will redeem my soul from the power of the grave: for
he shall receive me. Selah.
Psalm:49:15
Offer unto God thanksgiving; and pay thy vows unto the most
High:
Psalm:50:14
Whoso offereth praise glorifieth me: and to him that ordereth
his conversation aright will I shew the salvation of God.
Psalm:50:23
Purge me with hyssop, and I shall be clean: wash me, and I shall
be whiter than snow.
Psalm:51:7
Create in me a clean heart, O God; and renew a right spirit
within me.
Psalm:51:10
The sacrifices of God are a broken spirit: a broken and a contrite
heart, O God, thou wilt not despise.
Psalm:51:17
But I am like a green olive tree in the house of God: I trust in
the mercy of God for ever and ever.
Psalm:52:8

Oh that the salvation of Israel were come out of Zion! When God bringeth back the captivity of his people, Jacob shall rejoice, and Israel shall be glad.
Psalm:53:6
For he hath delivered me out of all trouble: and mine eye hath seen his desire upon mine enemies.
Psalm:54:7
Evening, and morning, and at noon, will I pray, and cry aloud: and he shall hear my voice.
Psalm:55:17
Cast thy burden upon the LORD, and he shall sustain thee: he shall never suffer the righteous to be moved.
Psalm:55:22

. . . .

In God I will praise his word, in God I have put my trust; I will not fear what flesh can do unto me.
Psalm:56:4
My heart is fixed, O God, my heart is fixed: I will sing and give praise.
Psalm:57:7
Unto thee, O my strength, will I sing: for God is my defence, and the God of my mercy.
Psalm:59:17

. . . .

Give us help from trouble: for vain is the help of man.
Psalm:60:11
Through God we shall do valiantly: for he it is that shall tread down our enemies.

Psalm:60:12

He only is my rock and my salvation; he is my defence; I shall not be greatly moved.

Psalm:62:2

In God is my salvation and my glory: the rock of my strength, and my refuge, is in God.

Psalm:62:7

. . . .

My soul shall be satisfied as with marrow and fatness; and my mouth shall praise thee with joyful lips:

Psalm:63:5

. . . .

O thou that hearest prayer, unto thee shall all flesh come.

Psalm:65:2

Thou hast caused men to ride over our heads; we went through fire and through water: but thou broughtest us out into a wealthy place.

Psalm:66:12

God be merciful unto us, and bless us; and cause his face to shine upon us; Selah.

Psalm:67:1

Sing unto God, sing praises to his name: extol him that rideth upon the heavens by his name JAH, and rejoice before him.

Psalm:68:4

The Lord gave the word: great was the company of those that published it.

Psalm:68:11

Blessed be the Lord, who daily loadeth us with benefits, even the God of our salvation. Selah.
Psalm:68:19
For the LORD heareth the poor, and despiseth not his prisoners.
Psalm:69:33
Let them be ashamed and confounded that seek after my soul: let them be turned backward, and put to confusion, that desire my hurt.
Psalm:70:2
For thou art my hope, O Lord GOD: thou art my trust from my youth.
Psalm:71:5
Let my mouth be filled with thy praise and with thy honour all the day.
Psalm:71:8
But I will hope continually, and will yet praise thee more and more.
Psalm:71:14
They shall fear thee as long as the sun and moon endure, throughout all generations.
Psalm:72:5
In his days shall the righteous flourish; and abundance of peace so long as the moon endureth.
Psalm:72:7
He shall have dominion also from sea to sea, and from the river unto the ends of the earth.
Psalm:72:8
He shall spare the poor and needy, and shall save the souls of the needy.

Psalm:72:13
He shall redeem their soul from deceit and violence: and
precious shall their blood be in his sight.
Psalm:72:14
Blessed be the LORD God, the God of Israel, who only doeth
wondrous things.
Psalm:72:18
And blessed be his glorious name for ever: and let the whole
earth be filled with his glory; Amen, and Amen.
Psalm:72:19

. . . .

My flesh and my heart faileth: but God is the strength of my
heart, and my portion for ever.
Psalm:73:26

. . . .

For God is my King of old, working salvation in the midst of
the earth.
Psalm:74:12
For promotion cometh neither from the east, nor from the west,
nor from the south.
Psalm:75:6
Vow, and pay unto the LORD your God: let all that be round
about him bring presents unto him that ought to be feared.
Psalm:76:11
Thou hast with thine arm redeemed thy people, the sons of
Jacob and Joseph. Selah.
Psalm:77:15

He caused an east wind to blow in the heaven: and by his power
he brought in the south wind.
Psalm:78:26
Turn us again, O God, and cause thy face to shine; and we shall
be saved.
Psalm:80:3
I removed his shoulder from the burden: his hands were
delivered from the pots.
Psalm:81:6
I am the LORD thy God, which brought thee out of the land of
Egypt: open thy mouth wide, and I will fill it.
Psalm:81:10

· · · ·

He should have fed them also with the finest of the wheat: and
with honey out of the rock should I have satisfied thee.
Psalm:81:16
I have said, Ye are gods; and all of you are children of the most
High.
Psalm:82:6
That men may know that thou, whose name alone is
JEHOVAH, art the most high over all the earth.
Psalm:83:18
Blessed is the man whose strength is in thee; in whose heart are
the ways of them.
Psalm:84:5
For the LORD God is a sun and shield: the LORD will give
grace and glory: no good thing will he withhold from them that
walk uprightly.
Psalm:84:11

I will hear what God the LORD will speak: for he will speak peace unto his people, and to his saints: but let them not turn again to folly.
Psalm:85:8
Yea, the LORD shall give that which is good; and our land shall yield her increase.
Psalm:85:12
For thou, Lord, art good, and ready to forgive; and plenteous in mercy unto all them that call upon thee.
Psalm:86:5
Among the gods there is none like unto thee, O Lord; neither are there any works like unto thy works.
Psalm:86:8
For who in the heaven can be compared unto the LORD? who among the sons of the mighty can be likened unto the LORD?
Psalm:89:6
And let the beauty of the LORD our God be upon us: and establish thou the work of our hands upon us; yea, the work of our hands establish thou it.
Psalm:90:17

. . . .

For he shall give his angels charge over thee, to keep thee in all thy ways.
Psalm:91:11
The righteous shall flourish like the palm tree: he shall grow like a cedar in Lebanon.
Psalm:92:12
The LORD on high is mightier than the noise of many waters, yea, than the mighty waves of the sea.

Psalm:93:4

Blessed is the man whom thou chastenest, O LORD, and
teachest him out of thy law;

Psalm:94:12

For the LORD is a great God, and a great King above all gods.

Psalm:95:3

Before the LORD: for he cometh, for he cometh to judge the
earth: he shall judge the world with righteousness, and the
people with his truth.

Psalm:96:13

A fire goeth before him, and burneth up his enemies round
about.

Psalm:97:3

Exalt the LORD our God, and worship at his holy hill; for the
LORD our God is holy.

Psalm:99:9

For the LORD is good; his mercy is everlasting; and his truth
endureth to all generations.

Psalm:100:5

For he hath looked down from the height of his sanctuary; from
heaven did the LORD behold the earth;

Psalm:102:19

To hear the groaning of the prisoner; to loose those that are
appointed to death;

Psalm:102:20

The LORD is merciful and gracious, slow to anger, and
plenteous in mercy.

Psalm:103:8

Bless the LORD, ye his angels, that excel in strength, that do his
commandments, hearkening unto the voice of his word.

Psalm:103:20
Who coverest thyself with light as with a garment: who
stretchest out the heavens like a curtain:
Psalm:104:2
My meditation of him shall be sweet: I will be glad in the
LORD.
Psalm:104:34

. . . . .

Sing unto him, sing psalms unto him: talk ye of all his wondrous
works.
Psalm:105:2
Saying, Touch not mine anointed, and do my prophets no
harm.
Psalm:105:15
And he saved them from the hand of him that hated them, and
redeemed them from the hand of the enemy.
Psalm:106:10
The earth opened and swallowed up Dathan and covered the
company of Abiram.
Psalm:106:17
They joined themselves also unto Baalpeor, and ate the sacrifices
of the dead.
Psalm:106:28

. . . .

Nevertheless he regarded their affliction, when he heard their
cry:
Psalm:106:44

He sent his word, and healed them, and delivered them from
their destructions.
Psalm:107:20
Through God we shall do valiantly: for he it is that shall tread
down our enemies.
Psalm:108:13
Let mine adversaries be clothed with shame, and let them cover
themselves with their own confusion, as with a mantle.
Psalm:109:29
The LORD hath sworn, and will not repent, Thou art a priest
for ever after the order of Melchizedek.
Psalm:110:4
He hath given meat unto them that fear him: he will ever be
mindful of his covenant.
Psalm:111:5
The fear of the LORD is the beginning of wisdom: a good
understanding have all they that do his commandments: his
praise endureth for ever.
Psalm:111:10
Wealth and riches shall be in his house: and his righteousness
endureth for ever.
Psalm:112:3

. . . .

Unto the upright there ariseth light in the darkness: he is
gracious, and full of compassion, and righteous.
Psalm:112:4
From the rising of the sun unto the going down of the same the
LORD's name is to be praised.
Psalm:113:3

He maketh the barren woman to keep house, and to be a joyful mother of children. Praise ye the LORD.
Psalm:113:9
The LORD hath been mindful of us: he will bless us; he will bless the house of Israel; he will bless the house of Aaron.
Psalm:115:12
For thou hast delivered my soul from death, mine eyes from tears, and my feet from falling.
Psalm:116:8
It is better to trust in the LORD than to put confidence in princes.
Psalm:118:9
They compassed me about like bees: they are quenched as the fire of thorns: for in the name of the LORD I will destroy them.
Psalm:118:12
The LORD is my strength and song, and is become my salvation.
Psalm:118:14
I shall not die, but live, and declare the works of the LORD.
Psalm:118:17
Blessed be he that cometh in the name of the LORD: we have blessed you out of the house of the LORD.
Psalm:118:26
Open thou mine eyes, that I may behold wondrous things out of thy law.
Psalm:119:18
Thy testimonies also are my delight and my counsellors.
Psalm:119:24
At midnight I will rise to give thanks unto thee because of thy righteous judgments.

Psalm:119:62
Thou through thy commandments hast made me wiser than
mine enemies: for they are ever with me.
Psalm:119:98
Thy word is a lamp unto my feet, and a light unto my path.
Psalm:119:105
The LORD shall preserve thy going out and thy coming in from
this time forth, and even for evermore.
Psalm:121:8
Pray for the peace of Jerusalem: they shall prosper that love
thee.
Psalm:122:6
Peace be within thy walls, and prosperity within thy palaces.
Psalm:122:7
Our help is in the name of the LORD, who made heaven and
earth.
Psalm:124:8
They that trust in the LORD shall be as mount Zion, which
cannot be removed, but abideth for ever.
Psalm:125:1
They that sow in tears shall reap in joy.
Psalm:126:5
He that goeth forth and weepeth, bearing precious seed, shall
doubtless come again with rejoicing, bringing his sheaves with
him.
Psalm:126:6
Except the LORD build the house, they labour in vain that
build it: except the LORD keep the city, the watchman waketh
but in vain.
Psalm:127:1

For thou shalt eat the labour of thine hands: happy shalt thou be, and it shall be well with thee.
Psalm:128:2
Many a time have they afflicted me from my youth: yet they have not prevailed against me.
Psalm:129:2
Let Israel hope in the LORD: for with the LORD there is mercy, and with him is plenteous redemption.
Psalm:130:7

. . . .

Arise, O LORD, into thy rest; thou, and the ark of thy strength.
Psalm:132:8
Behold, how good and how pleasant it is for brethren to dwell together in unity!
Psalm:133:1
Who giveth food to all flesh: for his mercy endureth for ever.
Psalm:136:25
I will worship toward thy holy temple, and praise thy name for thy lovingkindness and for thy truth: for thou hast magnified thy word above all thy name.
Psalm:138:2
Thou knowest my downsitting and mine uprising, thou understandest my thought afar off.
Psalm:139:2
O GOD the Lord, the strength of my salvation, thou hast covered my head in the day of battle.
Psalm:140:7

Bring my soul out of prison, that I may praise thy name: the righteous shall compass me about; for thou shalt deal bountifully with me.
Psalm:142:7

Cause me to hear thy lovingkindness in the morning; for in thee do I trust: cause me to know the way wherein I should walk; for I lift up my soul unto thee.
Psalm:143:8

Blessed be the LORD my strength which teacheth my hands to war, and my fingers to fight:
Psalm:144:1

My goodness, and my fortress; my high tower, and my deliverer; my shield, and he in whom I trust; who subdueth my people under me.
Psalm:144:2

Send thine hand from above; rid me, and deliver me out of great waters, from the hand of strange children;
Psalm:144:7

Great is the LORD, and greatly to be praised; and his greatness is unsearchable.
Psalm:145:3

Thy kingdom is an everlasting kingdom, and thy dominion endureth throughout all generations.
Psalm:145:13

The LORD openeth the eyes of the blind: the LORD raiseth them that are bowed down: the LORD loveth the righteous:
Psalm:146:8

He healeth the broken in heart, and bindeth up their wounds.
Psalm:147:3

For he hath strengthened the bars of thy gates; he hath blessed thy children within thee.
Psalm:147:13
He sendeth forth his commandment upon earth: his word runneth very swiftly.
Psalm:147:15
He sendeth out his word, and melteth them: he causeth his wind to blow, and the waters flow.
Psalm:147:18
Let them praise the name of the LORD: for his name alone is excellent; his glory is above the earth and heaven.
Psalm:148:13

. . . .

Let the high praises of God be in their mouth, and a two-edged sword in their hand;
Psalm:149:6
Let the saints be joyful in glory: let them sing aloud upon their beds.
Psalm:149:5
Praise ye the LORD. Praise God in his sanctuary: praise him in the firmament of his power.
Psalm:150:1
Let every thing that hath breath praise the LORD. Praise ye the LORD.
Psalm:150:6

Don't miss out!

Visit the website below and you can sign up to receive emails whenever Johannes Tefo publishes a new book. There's no charge and no obligation.

https://books2read.com/r/B-A-UEZX-UHTYC

BOOKS 2 READ

Connecting independent readers to independent writers.

Did you love *Times Getting Hard: Scriptures Of Comfort For Hard Days*? Then you should read *Identity In Christ*[1] by Johannes Tefo!

IDENTITY IN CHRIST

JOHANNES TEFO

2

Uncover who you truly are in Christ with "Identity in Christ"! This book helps you see yourself differently, with stories and easy-to-understand lessons. It's like a guide showing you how loved and special you are to God. You'll learn to be confident and find your purpose, feeling free from doubts and fears. If you're unsure about yourself or want to feel closer to God, this book is for you. Get ready to be inspired and discover the awesome

1. https://books2read.com/u/bzry0L

2. https://books2read.com/u/bzry0L

person you were meant to be. Dive into "Identity in Christ" now and start your journey to feeling whole and loved!

Also by Johannes Tefo

Family spiritual Warfare Books
Youth's Guide To Spiritual Warfare
A Women's Guide To Spiritual Warfare

Standalone
Deliver Your Soul From Evil
Overcoming Spirit Of Stagnation
The 24: Prophetic Word For This Season 2024 And Beyond
Michael For Warfare
Territorial Spirits: Overcome Evil Strongholds in Your Life And
Take Over Your Community With Strategic Warfare And
Winning Prayers
Prayers Against Suicide Spirit
Spiritual Warfare When Enough is Enough
Identity In Christ
Prayers Against Satanic Networks
The Workplace You Need: Spiritual Warfare Prayers That
Silence Evil Powers At Your Workplace.

Deliverance From Mind Control: Be Free And Delivered From Every Marine Demons Of Mind Control
Times Getting Hard: Scriptures Of Comfort For Hard Days

About the Author

Before he started writing Christian books, Johannes got a graduate degree in Film and Television from university of Johannesburg. After that, just to shake things up, he went to equip himself with religious studies, particularly Christianity, just to have knack about the world beyond the curtains of time. And how this body of Christ has transformed millions of people around the world, not neglecting how sadly the movement has been persecuted from time to time. He now writes full time.